Contents

Introduction   **6**

Chapter 1   Is Proud to Round Up a Varied Assortment **FOR OPENERS**   **8**

Chapter 2   Illustrates How This Book Is Already **GOING TO THE DOGS**   **32**

Chapter 3   Has a Habit of **MAKING FACES**   **46**

Chapter 4   Attempts to Put Together **A TRICKY ASSEMBLAGE**   **64**

Chapter 5   Is Nothing Less Than **THE CAT'S MEOW**   **82**

Chapter 6   Claims to Be a Gentle Treatise on **LOVE 'N' STUFF**   **100**

Chapter 7   Is Quick to Point Out Some of Life's **LITTLE INDIGNITIES**   **116**

Chapter 8   Takes Pleasure in Presenting **A PACK OF TRUNKS**   **142**

Chapter 9   Keeps an Ear Out for Some **CHOICE CHATTER**   **154**

Chapter 10   Sets Aside a Moment to Glance at Some **REAL SPORTS**   **174**

Chapter 11   Shows Appreciation for the Fine Art of **HORSING AROUND**   **194**

Chapter 12   Bids a Fond Farewell with This **MIXED BAG**   **208**

INTRODUCTION

When the forerunner of this book was published in 1987, LIFE SMILES BACK was such an instant success that Simon & Schuster immediately requested a sequel. Here it is— LIFE LAUGHS LAST—222 more funny photographs from the final page of America's favorite picture magazine. Titled *Miscellany*, this page has been used for years by LIFE to sign off each issue. It is designed to make the reader of the magazine, no matter what its content, conclude it with a smile or, better still, with a hearty laugh.

LIFE's editors have defined the *Miscellany* page in the following manner. "We consider humor the prime ingredient. The picture is usually a very simple one—an animal caught in a human predicament, a human trapped by the unexpected, a trick of the lens whereby a perfectly ordinary event recorded on film at just the right angle becomes ridiculous and thereby laughs out loud at all of us."

In plain words, on the pages ahead is an outlandish mixture of crazy doings, tangled limbs, weird sights, preposterous faces, lost perspectives, nutty places, fishy tears, improbable perils, minor disparagements, helping trunks, dogged cats, catty dogs and a lot of horsing around. Chimps, deer, mallards and a kangaroo are all part of the fun. As well as osculation escalation and invidious retribution. Can a first-grader do his studies with a lion breathing down his neck? Will a wedding happen under water? Is a jaywalking crate a hazard? Proceed at your own risk for the answers.

For the most part, the pictures that follow were taken by amateurs or by newspaper photographers with an eye cocked for the unexpected or the bizarre. The names of the people who took the pictures and the dates they originally appeared in LIFE are printed in small type right beside the photographs. You can blame me for the words. Occasionally a pun, an alliteration or a play on words is lifted straight out

In a 1953 issue of LIFE, this picture (without racquet) ran in a story entitled "Collegiate Cat." Reader Joan Houston of Smith College did some darkroom doctoring and came up with a feline tennis player. Pictures that have been tampered with like this one were not allowed to appear in this book. Allowed, though, were pictures that had the *Miscellany* humor but originally appeared elsewhere in the magazine.

of the original magazine, but most of the time the headlines and captions had to be newly conceived to marry pictures that had hardly met before. Information about the contents of each picture, usually long outdated, has been cut to the bone. And no tricks are revealed. By tricks I mean no tricks of the eye or the camera. This book has carefully kept away from those little cheaters that get their laughs from retouching or cut-and-paste techniques. Those images can be engaging but they are not real. They are cartoons. The difference between LIFE LAUGHS LAST and a book of cartoons is that all the sights here really happened. That makes them doubly funny.

There is something marvelously unpretentious about this collection of pictures. Here is a feast of spirited animals and beguiling children along with some unsuspecting grownups in for a surprise. The humor is basic—down to earth, simple, obvious—animals acting like people, older people acting like children, sudden indignities, the very large or the very small, more than one of the same thing, exaggerations, the incongruous, the impossible, somebody in a fix. We laugh, sometimes with relief, and we quickly show the pictures to others. While anger and sorrow are usually best experienced alone, humor is gregarious—we want to share what amuses us.

In the chapters that follow, the juxtapositions of the pictures are contrived to add to the humor. Our lives are filled with odd, unlikely combinations, but they are seldom frozen for us so that we can take joy in them.

In strange ways, this book of humor has its serious side. It shows our special relationship and affinity to other members of the animal kingdom. It makes us consider the paradoxes in our own lives. Its amusing, often tender glimpses somehow enlarge us and make us more human. And most important of all, it helps us not to take ourselves too seriously.

Often LIFE's contributors reconfirmed the authenticity of their pictures by keeping the editors updated on their children or pets. On page 34 you will find the classic photo of a German dog named Sepp on all fours carrying four cups and saucers on his nose (above). A few months after it was published, contributor D. Olin followed up with a second picture showing Sepp's progress. Now he could balance an even bigger snoutful standing on his hind legs.

Bettmann/UPI, 8/10/59

Chapter 1
Is Proud to
Round Up a
Varied Assortment
FOR OPENERS

Trying for Spilt Milk

During snack time at the zoo in Chessington, England, one chimp takes his refreshment straight up, the other gets his on the drops.

Passing the Buck

These Maryland hunters appear to be overarmed.

A German deer checks out his official autobahn crosswalk.

Coming

When three-year-old
Patrick Neukirch turned
around, one boot
obeyed, the other didn't.

If this is two spelunkers entering
a West Virginia cave, O.K.
If it's only one, Lesley Tarleton
has problems.

H.J. Neukirch, 2/23/62

or Going?

James E. Walczak, 8/22/55

Umbrella Policy

At West Germany's deluxe hotels there are valet services for practically everything.

Sylvian Corrodi, June 1980

Paul Kaye, 8/25/58

**During showers this thirsty cocker spaniel gets
under the nearest umbrella and drinks the runoff.**

When Duty Doesn't Call

When Terry Conant's friends paid him and his broken
leg a visit, their bedside manners were comical.

Roger Conant, 4/9/56

For this Swedish fire brigade, posing takes priority over hosing.

I.M.S., 6/19/64

An Austrian worker can't resist the tantalizing scent of newly baked bread.

Caught in the Act

A perfect time for a Mexico City pickpocket to pick.

Jenaro Olivares, Novidades, 5/1/50

George Silk, LIFE, 4/20/62

A Couple of Squirts

Swimmer Kathy Flicker is
neither here nor there.
Refraction of the water
has made her lose her head
and now Kathy has
no stomach for her mouth-
watering mouthful.

A Washington water sprite
makes like a fountain
at the Glen Echo
amusement park pool.

Mark Kauffman, LIFE, 9/7/53

Unguarded Rear Flank

Three-year-old Tracy Ann Hendry is so absorbed with feeding a goat she doesn't know what's eating her.

Shel Hershorn, Black Star, 11/10/61

A flower girl and her crafty accomplice work on a resale.

New Look of Patriotism

Rocco Morabito, *Jacksonville Journal, 10/21/57*

**At the Annie Beaman School in Jacksonville, Florida,
a guest joins the first-graders in the pledge of allegiance.
Hoppy wants liberty and justice for all rabbits too.**

**Taking liberties
with a lady, a
helicopter
momentarily
extinguishes her
welcoming flame.**

Pedaling Far-Eastern Wares

**In Vietnam a bike with a built-in honk helps
a goose farmer deliver his live haul to market.**

John A. Smith III, 3/4

26

In China members of the Acrobatic Art Theater ride a bicycle built for ten.

Keystone, 1/28/66

So What's New?

**In Claremont, California, a tree for a
new development is coerced into flight.**

John Duricka, San Gabriel Valley Tribune, 9/4/64

**In Jacksonville, Florida, a businessman greets a
rocket-suit tester high over the St. Johns River.**

It Was Bound to Happen

In Liberal, Kansas, water mess Gloria Good made with her tailgating!

Joe Cannon, 8/23/63

In Fort Worth, Texas, Donald Lee forgot his spare.

Raymond Dovel, 10/26/62

Chapter 2
Illustrates How This Book Is Already
GOING TO THE DOGS

Handy Paws

Peeking over the door of Raymond Dovel's car, this toy bullterrier named Cookie demonstrates some sleight of hand.

In Munich an Alsatian waiter named Sepp brings on coffee for four.

A Couple of Classics

Ron James, 2/19/65

It's fall in Michigan, the leaves are on the ground, and this Dalmation named Woody does his annual vanishing act.

Getting In Their Licks

A six-year-old pug named Sandora tries cherry.

Bettmann/Reuters, 8/17/53

A dog of dubious heritage tries child.

Studies in Dejection

Senator Sen-Sen is a three-year-old Chinese-crested who cries whenever Mrs. Frank Upton ignores her.

Loomis Dean, LIFE, 8/31/53

For this mournful Canadian basset, life is just too much.

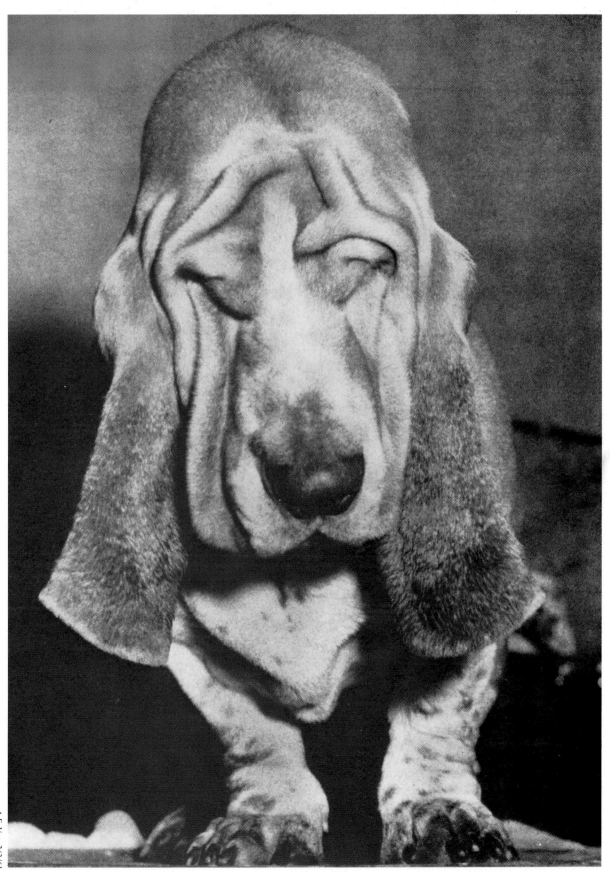

A.E. Van. 2/3/61

Putting On the Dog

A watchdog named Gustave is caught watching.

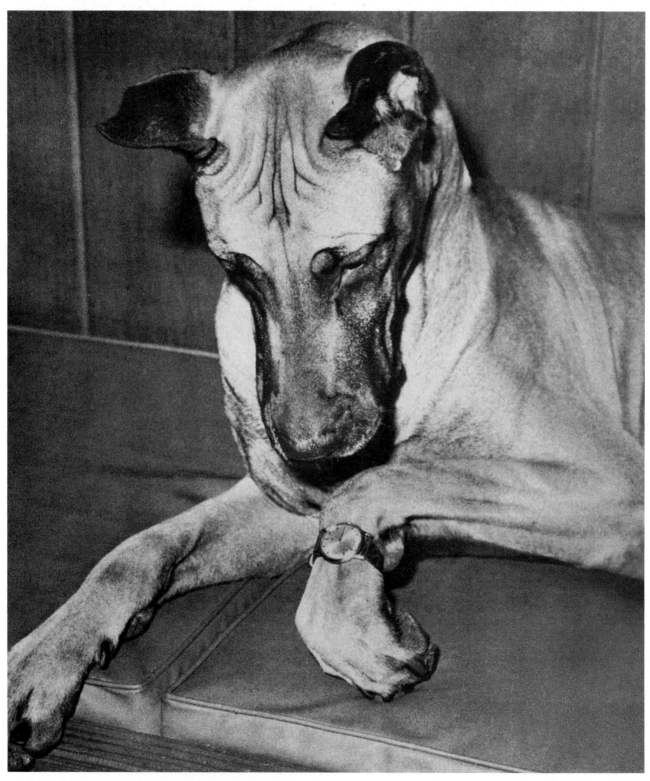

Art Ablire, 5/5/61

Oregon robins use this birdbrain for a landing strip.

John Ericksen, *Oregon Statesman*, 10/17/55

Snooty Affairs

Just before lunch Angus raps with the ratatouille.

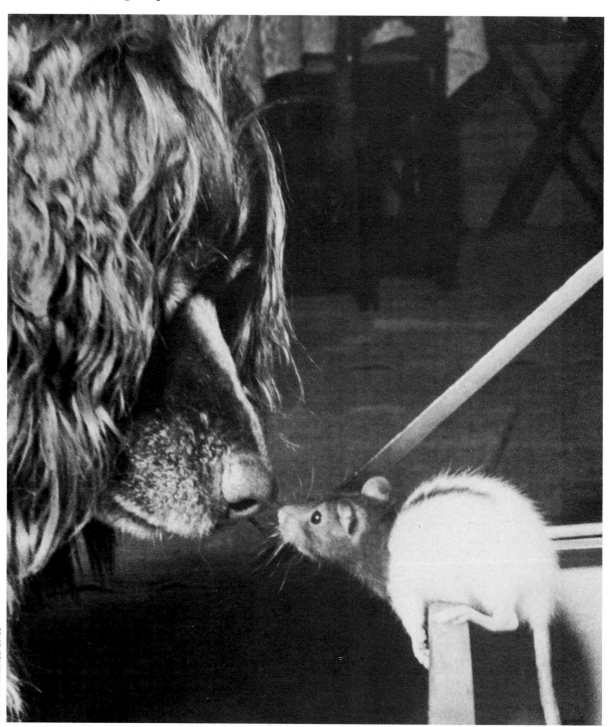

Arthur M. Uhlmann, 2/21/55

A St. Bernard named Hughie dreams of creamed chipped munk.

Fritz Connor, 10/20/61

Sinner or Saint?

Cheek to jowl, two Kansas bulldogs have a bone to pick.

Mrs. Barrett Van Dyke, 2/11/57

So beatific is this London bulldog that even his collar seems celestial.

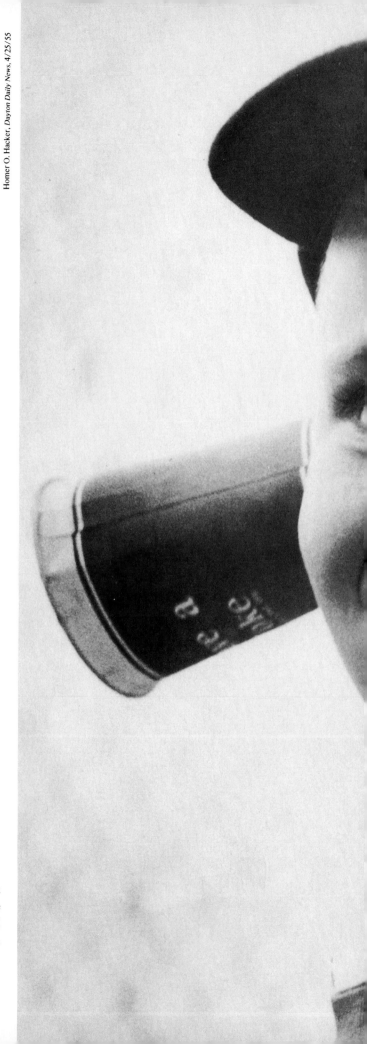

Chapter 3
Has a Habit of
MAKING
FACES

Homer O. Hacker, *Dayton Daily News,* 4/25/55

A Cutup
in His Cups

Nine-year-old Billy Foster tops off a
weird face by punching out the
bottoms of a couple of paper cups and
clamping them on his ears.

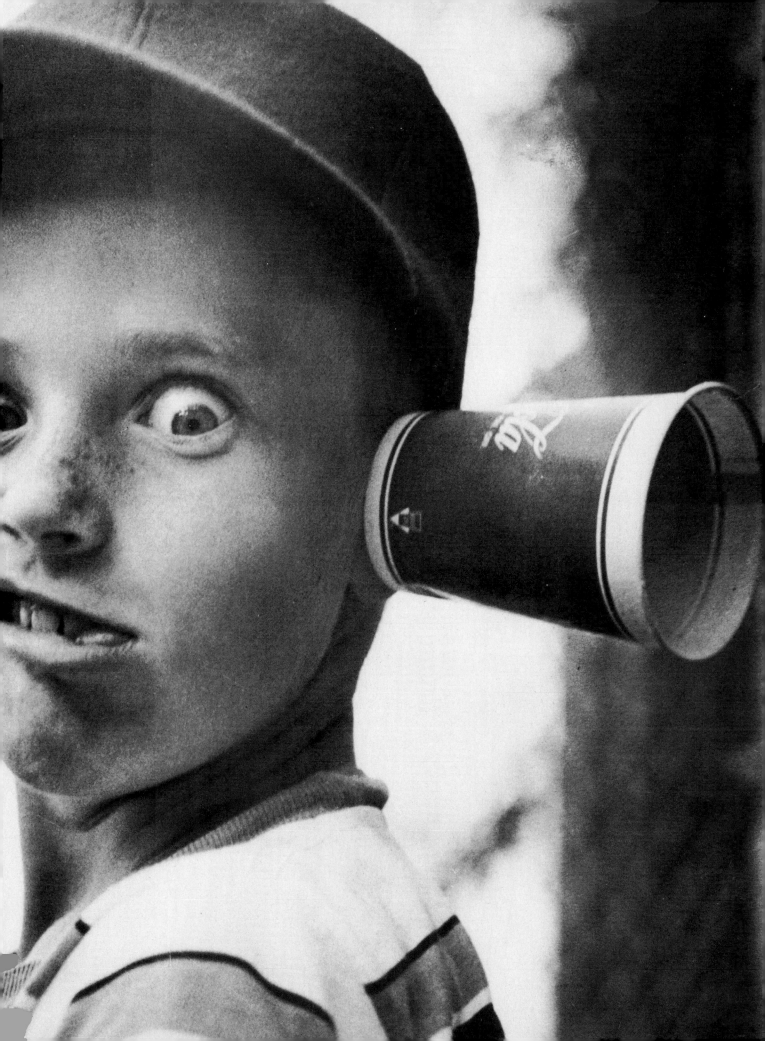

Acquired Tastes

Oysters were an unknown quantity to these Baltimore fifth-graders until
ten-year-old Donna Mikell finally got her courage up and popped one in. As she
goes for the swallow, classmate Eva Rigoupoulis looks on in sheer horror.

Walter McCardell, Baltimore Evening Sun, 10/20/58

This six-year-old orangutan in England's Bristol Zoo ponders whether or not to try the chicken.

Two-Faced Thingamabobs

This is the highly magnified top side of a half-inch-long bug of the order Hemiptera. Among other things, it sucks sap from plants and blood from animals. All the markings here are natural save for the nose, which is really the head of a pin impaling the carcass.

Andrzej Jan Wroblewski, 5/11/62

Francis Early, courtesy Casco Mills, 7/27/42

How would you like to bump into the Abominable Snowman some dark night? Back away and you'll see it's only the nose of a harmless guinea pig.

Abrupt About-Face

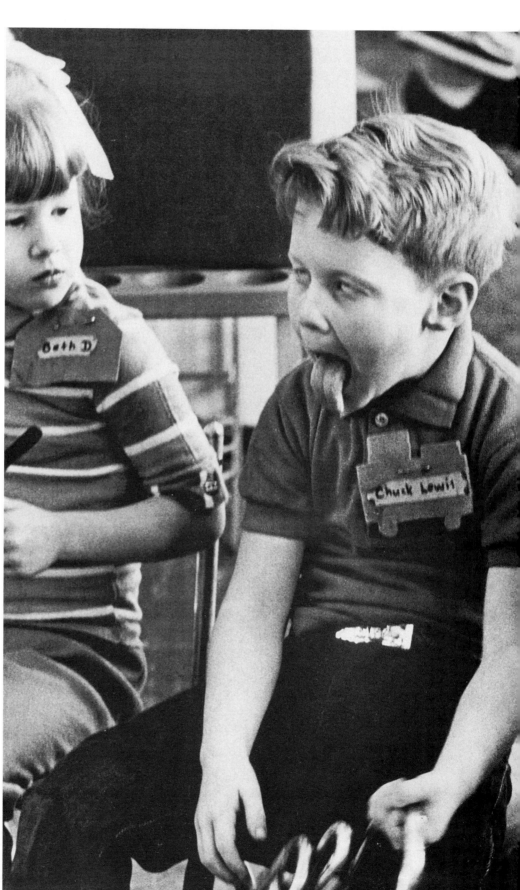

Ward Sharrer, 8/2/68

After regally posing for 20 straight minutes, Indiana beauty queen Esther Wood is told she can relax.

After tooting a solo, first trumpet Chuck Lewis wants everyone to know how taxing it was.

Alex Frechette, 11/13/39

Saving Face

In Florida, Flippy poses for his portrait, as artist Ottmar F. von Fuehrer gives evidence that he is a painter with a porpoise.

Losing Face

Korean karate specialist Bok Eung Lee smashes nine layers
of heavy roofing tiles with one blast of his poor dear visage.

SSG Lloyd Perkins, U.S. Army, 6/9/67

The Look of Contentment

**This usually rambunctious ram is letting Washington
rancher Doyle Goldy remove his wool in shear tranquillity.**

Dick Larsen, *Wenatchee World.* 7/29/57

At the Prague Zoo a blissful marsupial lolls on the grass and thanks his lucky stars he's in Czechoslovakia.

Hugo Vitamvas, *Camera Press*, October, 1984

In Oklahoma, Mrs.
Margorie Munson and
rooster hit high C in
a crowing contest.

Cornell Capa, LIFE, 1/26/48

With his 2½-year-old accompanist, Connie Meade, sounding
the note, Gato demonstrates why his nickname is Caruso.

the Music

Backstage at the Met, Minnie practices an aria.

In Los Angeles, Jerry warbles in falsetto.

Self-Inflicted Facials

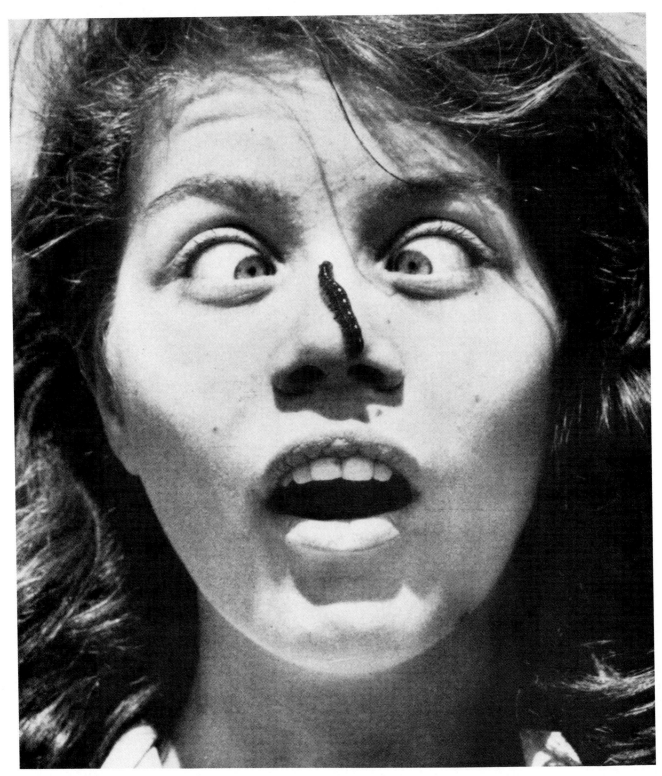

Earl Johnson, 6/9/52

During a caterpillar epidemic in Minnesota, ten-year-old Leota Hoaglun eyes one of the invaders crossly.

Jack Herod, *Los Angeles Times*, 3/16/42

**Little boys have made this face at Jiggs, so the
clownish orangutan from Hollywood makes it right back.**

Fake Face to Practice On

At the American Barber College in Los Angeles, before the students are allowed to try their skill on human volunteers, they practice on balloons fixed up to look like human faces. Often the results are explosive!

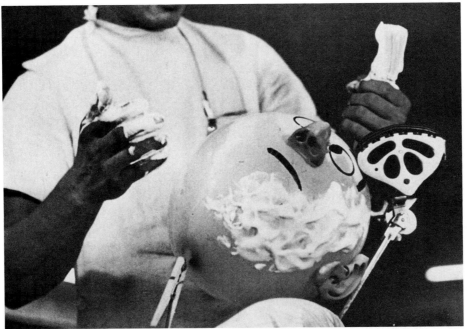

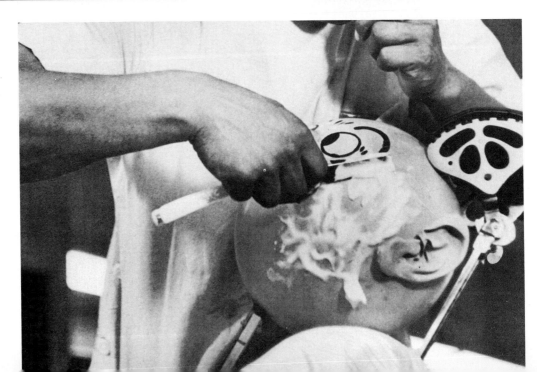

Chapter 4
Attempts to Put Together
A TRICKY ASSEMBLAGE

Pane in the Neck

A headless man carries glass in Paris.

Rene Maltete, Black Star, 1/5/62

Crowning Touches

When a storm knocked the head off this statue, 13-year-old Paul Jarvis was drafted to squeeze down the neck and tighten some loose bolts. For a moment, anyway, Vancouver had a heroic Bible-reading circuit rider with a pea head.

Tony Bacon, 1/3/64

Nine-year-old Mike Thwaites just loves getting in sister Josephine's hair

Fender Benders

Heels over head in work, this San Diego mechanic must be a dummy.

When he's fixing his truck, Vermont's Sonny Tadwell always gets headstrong.

Gladys W. Estabrook, 7/17/64

Kooky Crossings

Freeway motorists in Hutchinson, Kansas,
get a load of a house with a high overhead.

Frank Santiago, 10/22/65

Sidewalk strollers in London clap eyes on a couple of jaywalking crates.

London Daily Mirror, 6/2/'67

Long-Standing Uprights

Lee Balterman, 5/15/64

A Chicago beam that catches the eye.

Ralph Montali, 6/28/63

**A San Francisco mast
that's really stacked.**

During football, Georgia's Rex Evatt never lets his head get out of hand.

Wolf Lebovitz, *Chattanooga Times*, 11/27/50

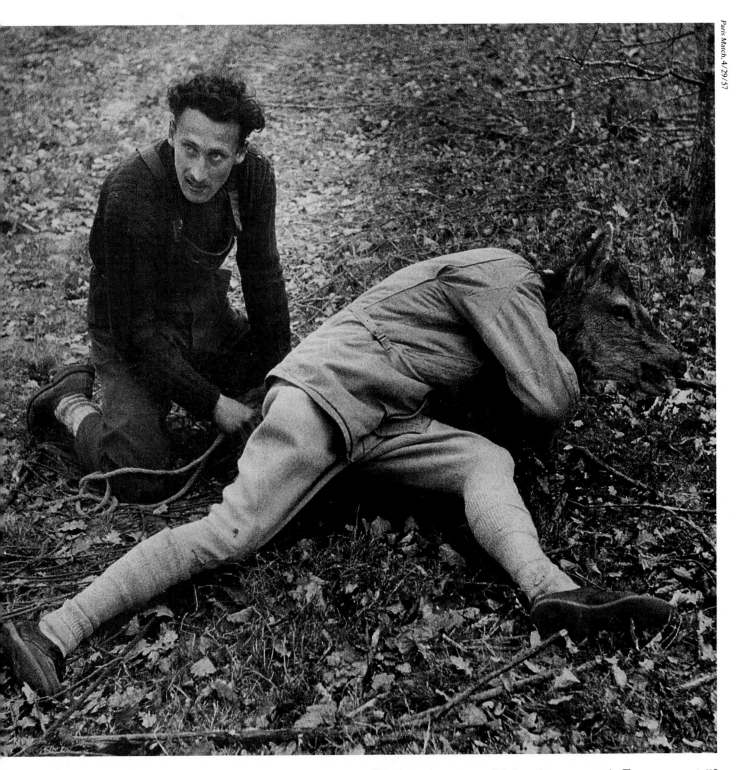

What creatures roam this hunting preserve in France, pray tell?

A Head of the Game

Constricting Construction

These Moscow balconies offer a rare degree of privacy.

Peter Worthington, 1/7/66

These Washington staircases provide easy access—but to where?

Walking on Water

For this energetic Briton swabbing the waves, the tide may
be just barely concealing the surface of a dry-dock cradle.

Guy Gravett, 4/11/55

For this muscled American, a
ripple may be disguising
a rock on which his handstand
might be resting.

Randy McKay, 8/24/59

Bettmann/UPI, 7/21/47

**For lovely Rosemary Preston, the smooth
river may be only an inch deep.**

GUESS WHO FALLS IN!

IT'S ROSEMARY-BABY!!!!

Bettmann/UPI, 7/21/47

Chapter 5
Is Nothing Less Than
THE CAT'S MEOW

Uncouth Cat

Liberated from outmoded ideas of feline grace, this flaked-out specimen
in Brattleboro, Vermont, listens to the jukebox and scowls at customers.

Fat Cats

Having inherited 365 pounds sterling from his departed British mistress,
Joseph is converting his currency into a heavier pound—so far 28 of them.

**Resting his sizable self on the arm of a New York City
apartment chair, Randy is taking 40 winks—39 to go.**

Ron Thompson. 8/20/65

No Room for Scaredy-Cats

This pole cat is the pride of Engine House No. 37 in Roxbury, Massachusetts.

This daring airborne evacuation from roof to tree to ground took place four times, all successful, as a Knoxville mama went out on a limb for her four 21-day-old kittens.

Mickey Craeger / Knoxville News Sentinel. 5/9/60

Skillful Attacks by Dogged Cats

**A Mexican dachshund cowers beneath a chair,
wondering where Trudy's next pounce will come from.**

Frank Scherschel, LIFE, 9/23/46

After ducking through a hole in the fence, Slippers
moves in to box the ears of he who dared to follow.

Milk of Human Kindness (Care of Cow)

A straight-shooting dairy farmer shows compassion for a thirsty barnyard friend.

Temper! Temper!

**Almost catatonic over his long wait for a
fish head, Simba tears into his weekly treat.**

Keystone, 1/11/54

In a New York cat show, Jet takes offense when a polite
little kitten named Charley Chan is named "most intelligent."

Nat Fein, New York Herald Tribune. 12/27/48

Embraceable who?

Improbable Pals

Well-guarded giggle

94

Orphans under wing

Keystone, 10/24/60

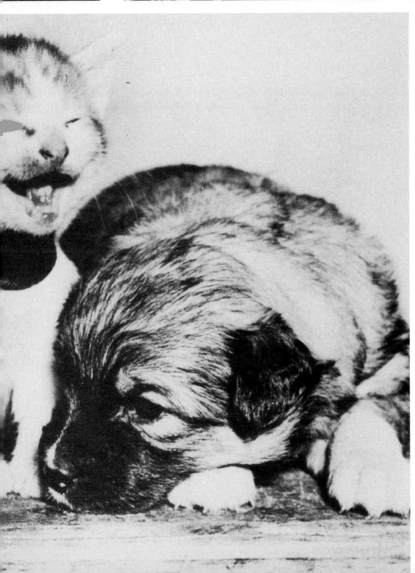

Bettmann/N.Y. Mirror, 5/6/40

Pussy's in the Well

Cleo is relaxing in her favorite hiding place.

Hedgecoth Photographers, 2/23/59

Saki Fats is making a billiard table catty-cornered .

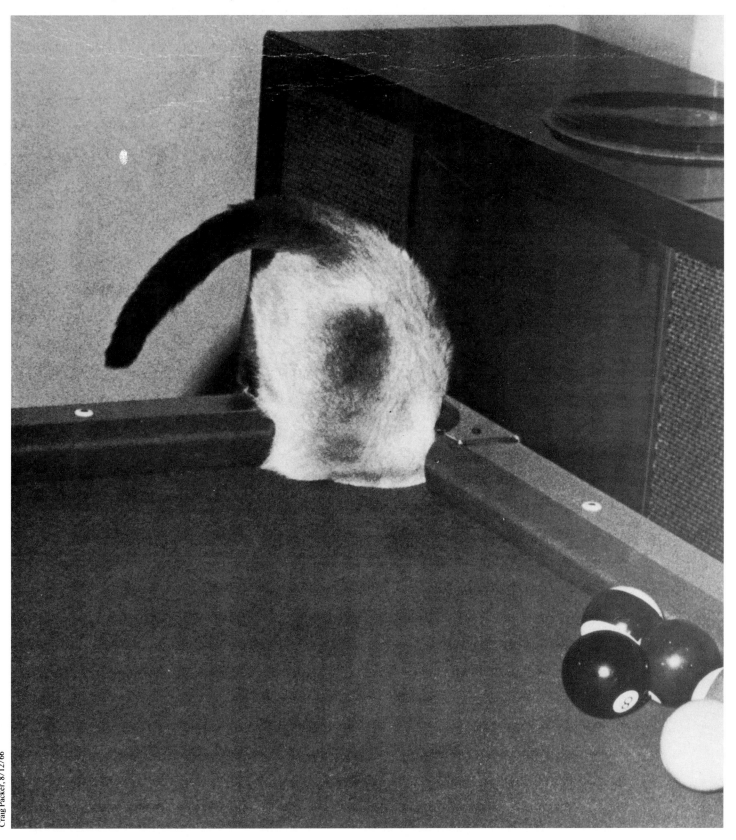

Craig Packer, 8/12/66

97

Vying for Attention

Archie does an entrechat but Puddy has no interest.

George Adams/ Dayton Journal-Herald, 3/24/61

Aida does a shimmy but now it's Rollo's turn to act blasé.

Zdenek Pivecka, 3/9/53

Chapter 6
Claims to
Be a Gentle
Treatise on
LOVE 'N' STUFF

We Can't Go On Meeting Like This

In front of a bus stop in Cincinnati, this couple has time to waste.

Thought-Provoking Sculpture

New York City patrolman Peter Witkus casts a
quizzical eye at the bare truth in Central Park.

In New York City's Museum of Modern Art, 3½-year-old
Louisa Waber muses over the future.

Bernard Waber, 11/2/59

Young Man's Fancy

Snuggling on a park bench in Prestwick, England, 17-year-old Paul Barton and his companion, Denza, turned nary a passing head— until one of them barked.

Osculation Escalation

Gruntly, a couple of romantic pigs exchange a rooting smooch.

Waiting to be released in the Thames, a pair of London swans bill and coo behind the back.

Wide World, 2/1/37

Gene Wolfsheimer, 4/7/52

You can see right through the advances of the tropical gourami, which come equipped with translucent lips.

Born in Moscow and raised in London, Sam and Sally enjoy a bear-faced embrace.

The Keystone Collection, 6/29/62

Graphic Photo Union, 8/20/51

In a South African zoo a lady hippo gratefully greets a new male suitor.

Wide World, 4/4/49

Paying Lip Service

This giraffe named Soeren is only five hours old but already he's partial to necking.

While collecting his trophy from beauty queen Valerie Grant, auto racer Jack Penwell prepares to give the cameraman some lip.

Jim Lucas, *Daily Oklahoman,* 8/1/60

Members of the Wedding

**Deep beneath her crinoline, something comes undone, so Margaret
Herzog's wedding consultant sets off on an errand of mercy.**

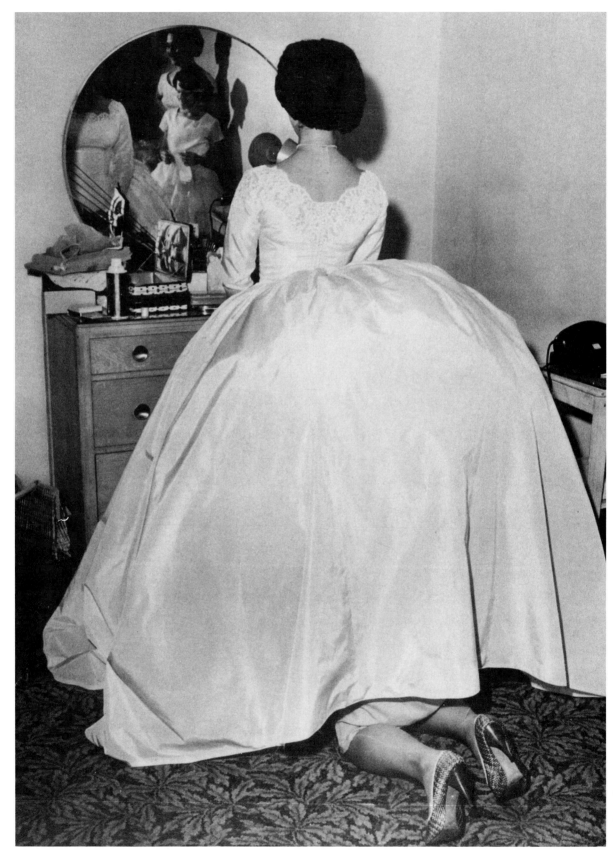

After checking out the something old, new, borrowed and blue in Sandra Leslie's bridal getup, eight-month-old wedding guest Howard Kruger comes up for air.

Nutty Places for Tying the Knot

On the very spot where they first met, diving clown Bob Smith takes aquamaid Mary Beth Sanger for better or worse—eight feet underwater.

John Dominis, LIFE, 3/8/54

In Ohio, flagpole sitter
"Mac Marshall" Jacobs and
Lonnie Cosmar get hitched by
loudspeaker, 176 feet up.

In France, this well-balanced
couple await the benediction
from a priest on a fire ladder.

J. Dieuzaide, 6/7/54

113

Talk About Taking the Plunge!

With the pilot shouting the service up to them, Garry Meddock and Tamara Ketham of Dayton, Ohio, get spliced atop his balloon.

David Kohl, May 1981

After tossing her bridal bouquet from the roof of her parent's poolhouse in San Jose, California, Robin Huzar follows suit.

Guy Marshall Anderson, February 1982

Chapter 7
Is Quick
to Point Out
Some of
Life's
LITTLE
INDIGNITIES

Distress over a Downfall

In a Minneapolis perambulator parade, 20-month-old Susan Baron is mortified by an elastic that let her down.

117

School Ties

Taking to the floor to protest opening day of school, Kansas first-grader Tommy Courter shows his low opinion of higher education.

Wilbur Hess, *Lawrence Journal World,* 10/5/62

How can you work with a lion breathing down your neck?

Music Critics

Three-year-old Lynne Jones gives her candid opinion of an amateur band in Maryland.

C.A. Hebbel, 9/9/57

Two-year-old Jodi Rae Walker gives her lowest mark to this noisy Oklahoma band.

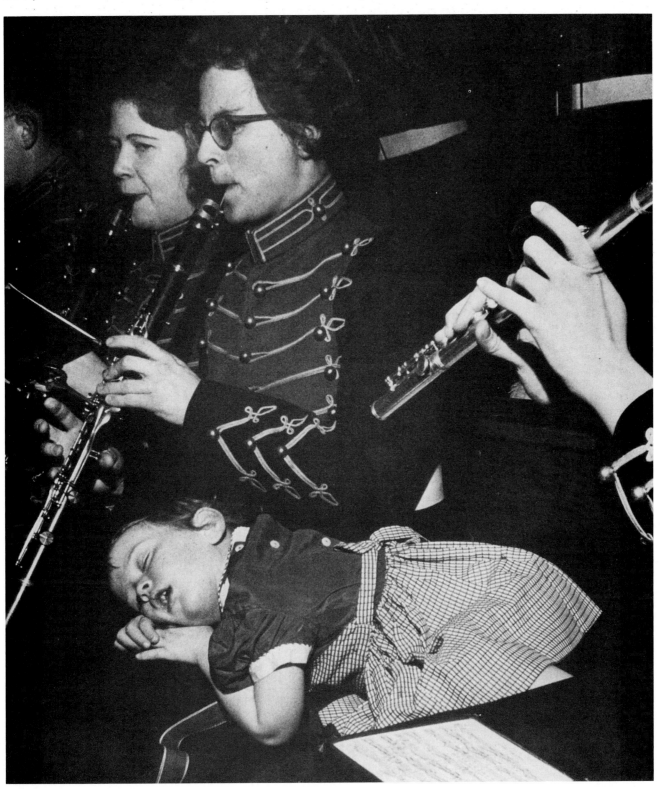

Allen J. Bird, 5/19/61

Stern Penalty for Standing

Odd angle for an angler to angle at.

I.M.S., 5/27/66

All ashore that's going ashore?

Ricardo J. Ferro, *St. Petersburg Times*, 5/10/68

**This ticketless Stockholm suburbanite will
go to any lengths to make his train.**

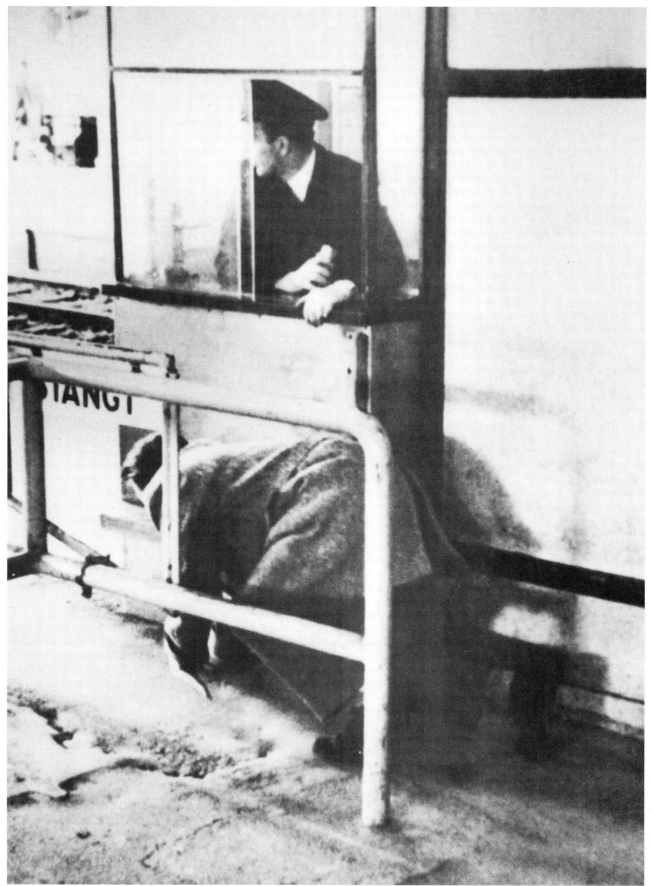

Commuting Woes

A New York subway rider leaves a footnote to a fast exit.

Bettmann/UPI, 10/24/69

A determined bull tries to outskirt a visitor.

for Dear Life

Hiding behind a mother's skirt these days can be difficult.

Pantomimes

In San Francisco, John Guilfoy is all thumbs trying to dress in public after a hotel fire drives guests from their rooms.

Ted Needham, *San Francisco Examiner*, 9/21/53

**In London, high-living Raymon Schaller uses
a trampoline to vault into his trousers.**

Tom Hustler, 2/22/60

Sitter Solutions

Improvisation in the park
brings momentary peace.

Pinning down her new job, Specs waits for further orders.

Eileen "Bonnie" Roberts, 2/9/62

Limited Vision

During a cloudburst, baggers can't be choosers.

Richard Pruitt, *Dallas Morning News*, 10/3/69

With the help of the upstate New York wind, this graduating
senior at Ithaca College has suddenly lost her perspective.

Perils
of the
Journey

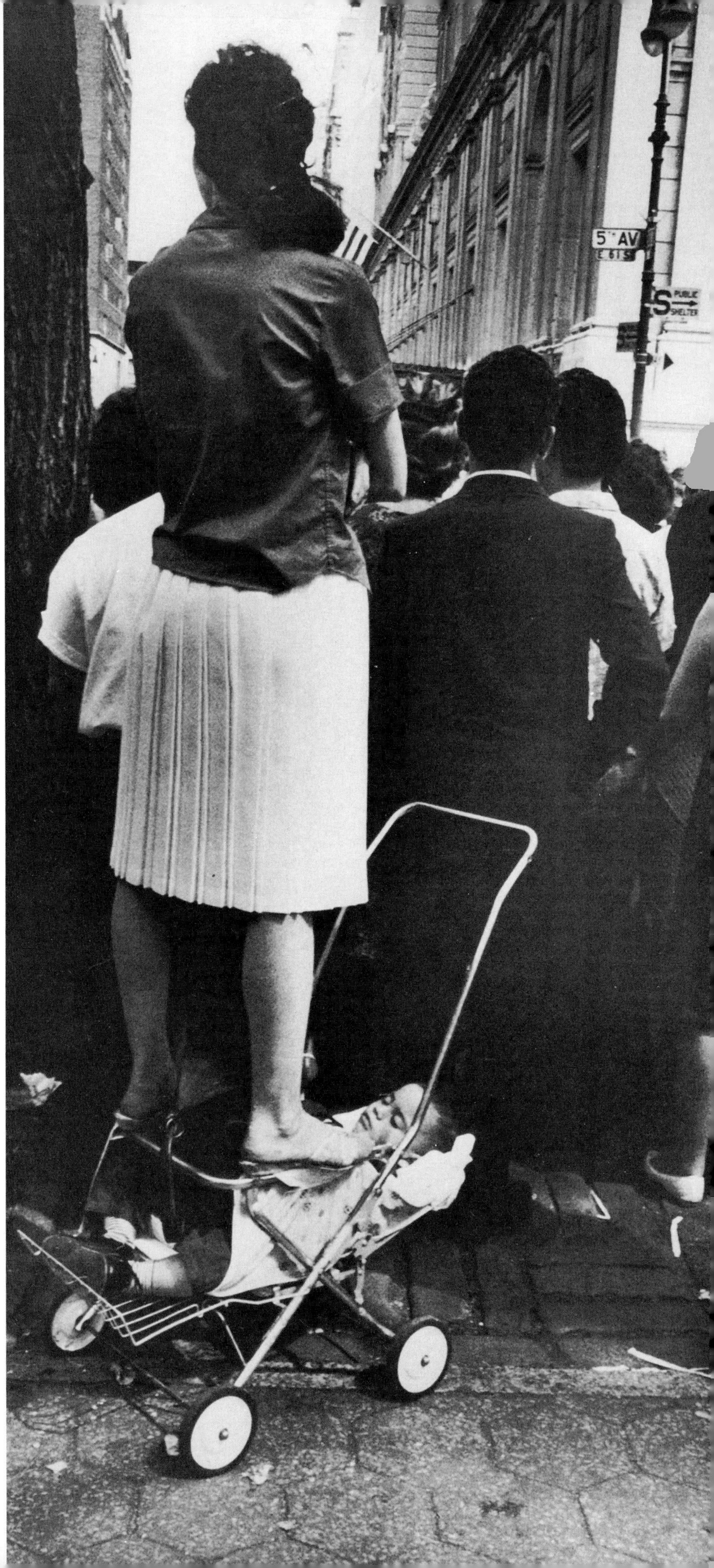

A Fifth Avenue parade puts extra stress on a stroller.

John Benton Harris, 8/30/63

134

While his mother is hung up checking the luggage, her fellow traveler waits to get off the hook.

Military

In a hard-fought nasal battle, this Korean cadet fights off a sneeze.

Matt McVay, Seattle Times, April 1980

Mishaps

Navy chaplain Captain Roy Bishop shakes off a sharp migraine and struggles through another ceremony.

Petrified Patients

Worried patient and empathetic master in a vet's waiting room.

Sea-going patient with an aching jaw.

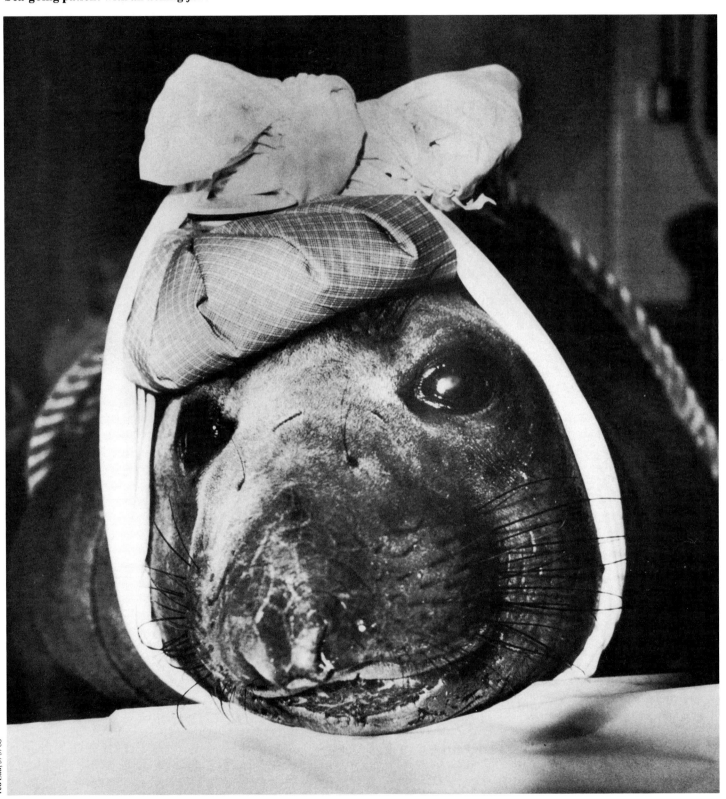

Shameless
Lamentation

There's nothing fishy
about his tears; Jon Beers
just doesn't like holding
his father's catch.

Since Douglas Kelley can't shut up his younger brother, he shuts him out instead.

Chapter 8 Takes Pleasure in Presenting

Art Rogers. 7/28/67

Area Code: Zoo

There's trouble on the trunk line. San Francisco can't get through to Paris.

A PACK OF TRUNKS

Tony Arnold, February 1988

The Nose Has It

Gypsy snorkels at Silver Springs, Florida.

Village Scenes

By noon the parking lot of the King's Arms Pub is almost full.

Keystone. 1/27/67

A helpful British attendant is on foot to give a stalled car a push.

John Drysdale, *Camera Press*, Winter 1978

147

Circus Chums' Day Off

This little stick-in-the-mud from Boswell's Circus needed a helping trunk from an elder to free him from the South African river ooze.

Gwen A. Hopkins, 5/17/54

Relaxing at the Oklahoma winter grounds of the Miller
Bros. Circus, Daisy's telling Myrtle not to be so snooty.

At Billy Smart's Circus in England, Gilda copies three-year-old Gary Jann—or vice versa.

London Daily Mirror 12/7/62

Headdownsmanship

At the Bertram Mills Circus, also in England, Sheila gets an "alley-oop" from Marina, the daughter of the bareback star.

Fox Photos, 2/26/65

Pachyderm Pranks

At the Toledo zoo in Ohio, a preoccupied keeper gets his sneaker chomped.

At the Six Flags over Texas amusement park near Dallas,
Charlene Wise shows concern for her necklace—and her neck.

Clint Grant, *Dallas Morning News*. 5/22/64

Chapter 9
Keeps an Ear Out for Some
CHOICE CHATTER

"Give Me a Break, Kid!"

In the Masai Mara Reserve in Kenya, a lion-hearted cub tries out his new teeth on Daddy's old hide.

"God's Truth, Judge. There Was This

A set-up job in San Francisco's Superior Court, Judge John Benson
presiding. In the witness chair three-month-old Jake Levy is appealing.

Guy on This Motorcycle and . . ."

Edward Barbee of Columbia, Missouri, is a motorcycle salesman with a slight disadvantage.

Rick Levy, August 1982

"It's Too Big to be a Cinder, Sir!"

Danny Gorman of Ardsley, New York, lets Cindy flip his lid.

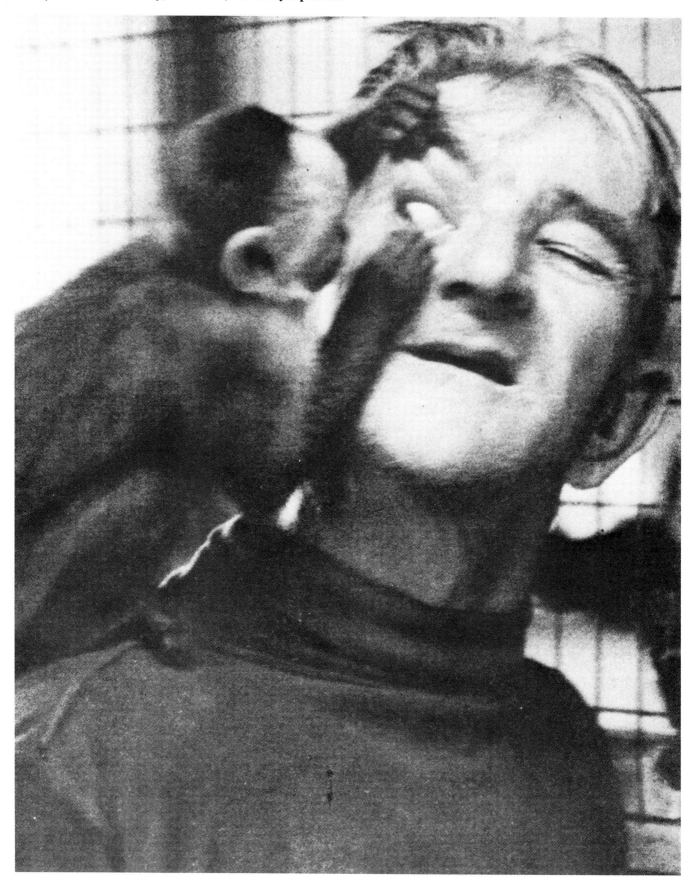

N.J. Harrick, 1/21/57

Charles Mentzer feels like a Cyclops as nurse Joan Ferris prepares to remove what's hurting.

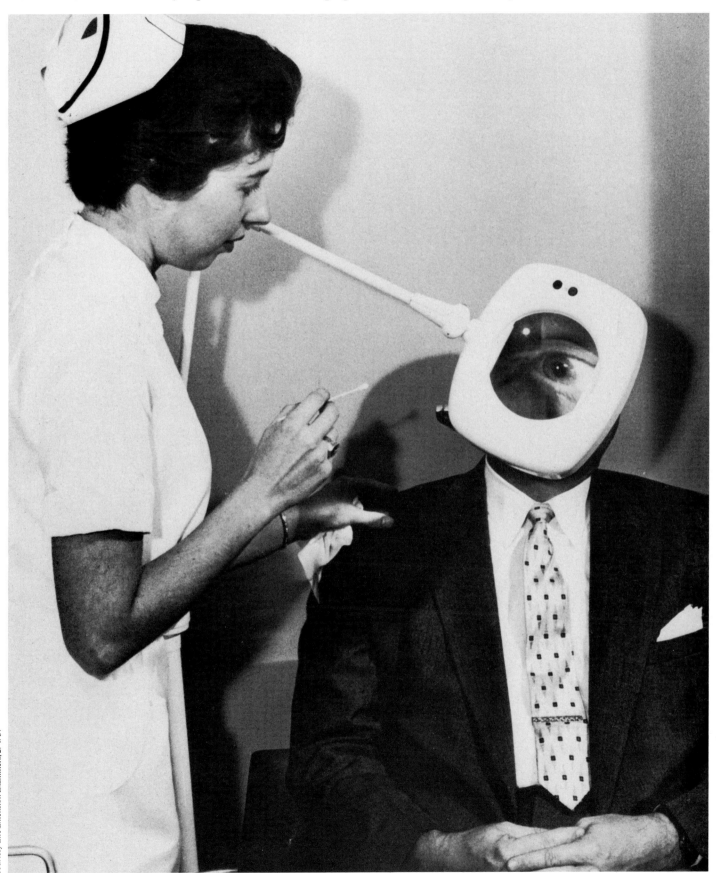

courtesy Life Extension Examiners, 2/4/57

"He Doesn't Talk." "His Head's Too Long."
"And Besides that, He Can't Keep a Straight Line."

Three Padaung
women pass
judgment on a
Grenadier Guard.

The thin red line
gets bent a little
as Guardsmen
rehearse for the
Queen's Birthday.

Bettmann/UPI, 7/30/71

A pair of Florida tree frogs named Freddie and May strut their stuff.

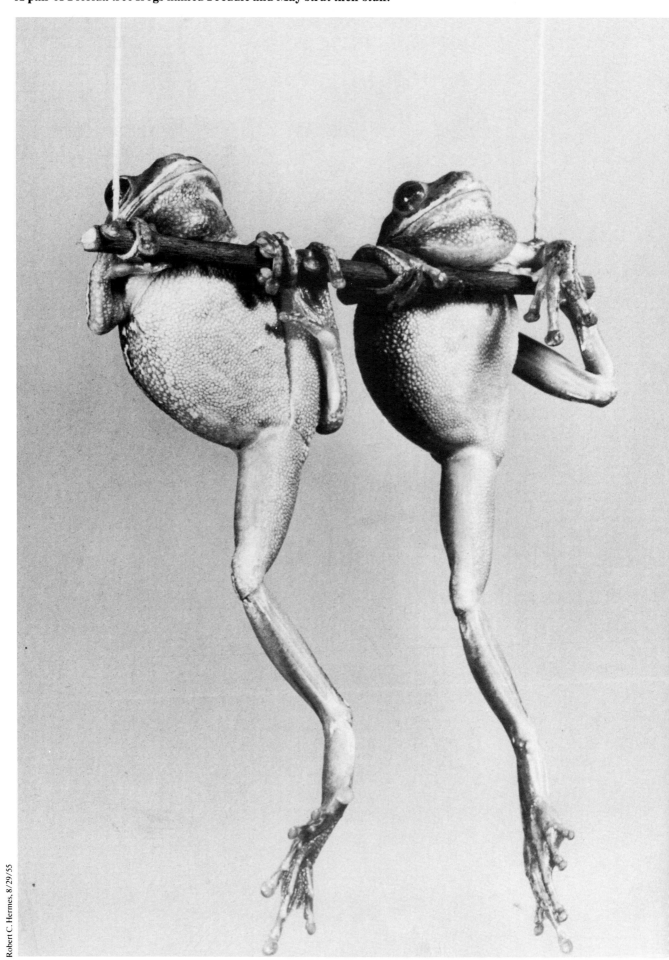

"Ya Put the Left Foot Forward and the Right Foot Back . . ."

A brace of antelopes practice a soft-shoe routine during lunch.

Norman Myers, 5/9/69

"Whenever You're Ready!"

A ground squirrel patiently waits for Stan Kazmiruk to change lenses.

Len Fertuck, 7/30/65

The telephone repairman is checking a dead line.

Keith Williams, *Henderson Gleaner*, 6/6/69

"Ho! Ho! Ho! . . . Hum! Hum! Hum!"

At the Amsterdam zoo, the horselaughs come with stripes.

Paul de Cordon, 3/16/62

At Cucamonga, California, a troika of basset hounds sniffs out the loopholes.

"This Gal Shows Promise!"

A sea lion named Charlie shamelessly ogles Betty Lauerman as she bares her charms for the camera.

Don Renn, 12/13/63

A weimaraner indicates his approval of twelve-year-old Joyce Rodgers.

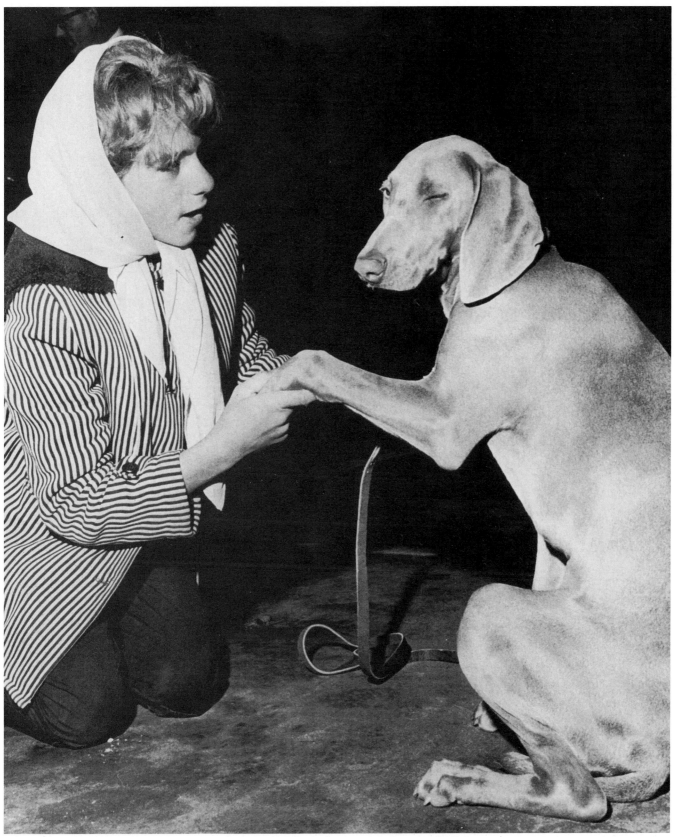

**This picture of a painting class at the Brooklyn Museum
School of Art attracted model applicants by the score.**

"Don't Voice It Around, but the New One Has a Definite Problem"

Around a conference table, there is musing over what a work of art is man.

Maris Engel, 1/12/68

"How Do I Get Outa Here?"

In Norfolk, Virginia, Leon Smith tries to pull himself out of a hole in the street.

In Pittsburgh, Pennsylvania, a part-collie named Butch finds his way through an abandoned water main to a hole in the sidewalk.

MISCELLANY

Orby G. Kelley, Jr., 11/24/58

La Salle Daily News Tribune, 9/3/65

In Waterloo, Iowa, Bossy has a long face after eating a barrel of apples.

No Credit, 1/

Near Spring Valley, Illinois, a Black Angus steer and farmer Louis Budnick puzzle over the horns of a dilemma.

In Titusville, Pennsylvania, a heifer plunked into the shaft of an abandoned well.

Yellowstone Park garbage dispose-all.

Bill Browning, 6/24/66

At an unknown location, a badger with a compulsive appetite is canned.

By the Way, They All Got Out Just Fine

Bishop C. Cornwell, Jr., 11/22/63

Chapter 10

Sets
Aside
a
Moment
to
Glance
at
Some

REAL SPORTS

Just Kick the Ball, Please!

Tulane's David East places a punt so perfectly you'd think the ball had eyes on it (to say nothing of legs and arms).

Elusive Prey

In Sussex, England, Wrong-Way Reynard outwits his adversaries.

In the forest of Fontainebleau, a hounded stag makes a surprise escape.

Delcourt, 1/29/65

177

Official Put-Downs

Faked out of his shoes by the Baylor ball runner, Texas Christian
end Buddy Iles puts the right tackle on the wrong guy.

Al Panzera, *Ft. Worth Star-Telegram,* 12/8/61

Critical of his eyesight, baseball fan Lucille Case marches onto the diamond and offers umpire Al Somers the use of her glasses. In a knee-jerk response, Somers gives her the thumb.

Bob Campbell, *San Francisco Chronicle, 5/26/52*

Sitting Ducks

**In Kansas, shooting sitting ducks is forbidden. All
this cagey mallard had to do was wait the hunters out.**

Peter R. Czura, 1/17/64

**Donald likes nothing better than being retrieved by Trigger.
Sometimes they play their little game a dozen times a day.**

Loomis Dean, LIFE, 8/1/49

End of the Road

Executing a "wheelie," Roine Loeow of Sweden almost executes himself.

Torsten Malmberg, I.M.S., 1/17/55

At California's Pomona College a half-miler flosses at the finish line.

Dave Meiklejohn, *Pomona Progress Bulletin*, 5/4/42

Sit-Down Strikes . . .

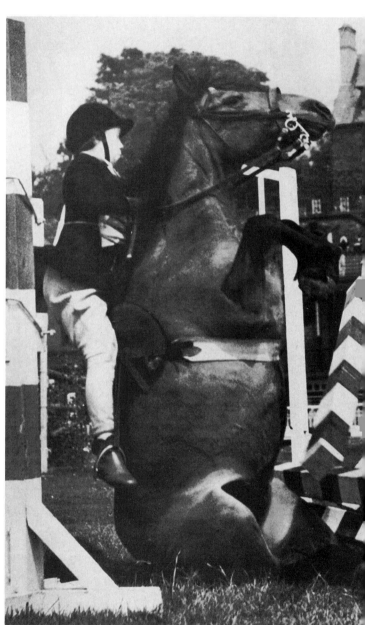

Jerry Frutkoff, 12/20/68

Enough of this run, run, run.

To heck with this jump, jump, jump.

184

...And a Scab

John Walker, 6/28/54

Keystone, 5/21/65

Colin Newlove and mount clear a barrier in Yorkshire.

Lars Speyer, 5/16/60

Classic Stances

Her flying follow-through almost bowls her over, but this California roller
knocks down her two remaining pins while balancing on only one of her own.

His spread-eagle dismount isn't normal procedure for
English steeplechasing, but hanger-on Peter Crouch made
it back aboard and actually crossed the finish line.

Muscle Power

**Missouri flood waters plunge this sign-
board swimmer right into his element.**

**While dancing the _zebekiko,_ a Greek
squid fisherman lets his table go to his head.**

Winter Madness

This Finn is realizing he's a skier at cross-purposes and probably finished.

**Hitting a "thank you, Ma'am" at top speed,
Barbara and Sue rise to the occasion.**

Richard Hunter, 1/13/61

Everybody's Doing It Every Which Way

Using unmatched skis, a girl does it at Florida's Cypress Gardens.

Using monster skis, an elephant does it in the Hudson River.

Using shorty skis, a squirrel does it at Sanford, Florida.

Using normal skis and carrying his shoes around his neck, commuter Don Ibsen does it in Seattle's Lake Washington.

Mitch Kezar, January 1980

Marshall Lockman, 8/12/57

Bettmann/N.Y. Mirror, 4/28/58

Linda A. LaMarre, 9/24/65

Come On, Just One Bite

This apple-polisher named Tic Toc wants to share 50-50 with his reluctant owner, Carol LaMarre.

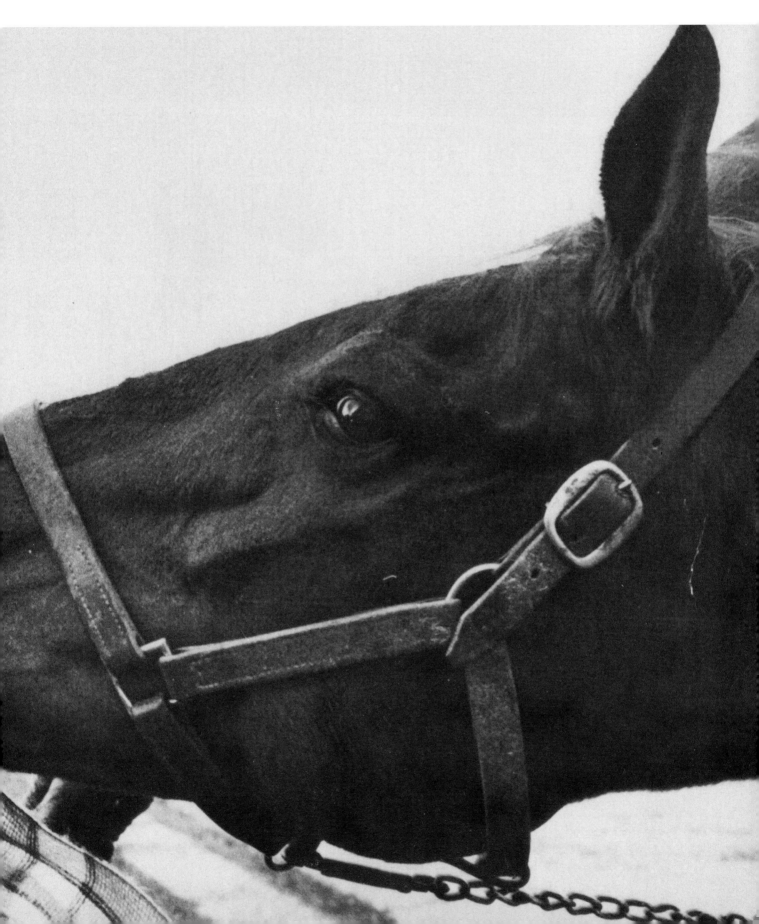

Mystifying Legwork

A spiffily shod Maryland hunter has a mixed gait.

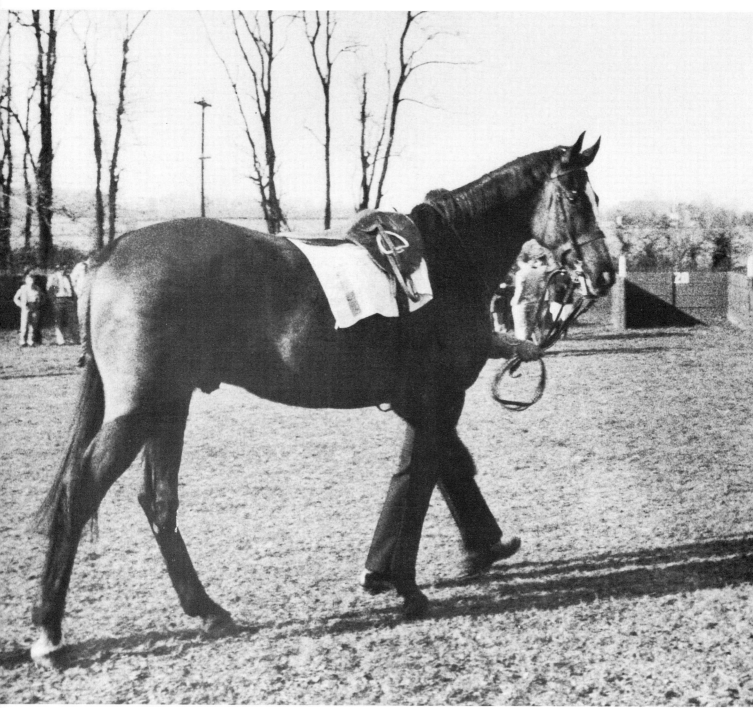

Julie Finette Davis, 11/11/5

This Italian speedster has somehow lost half his horsepower.

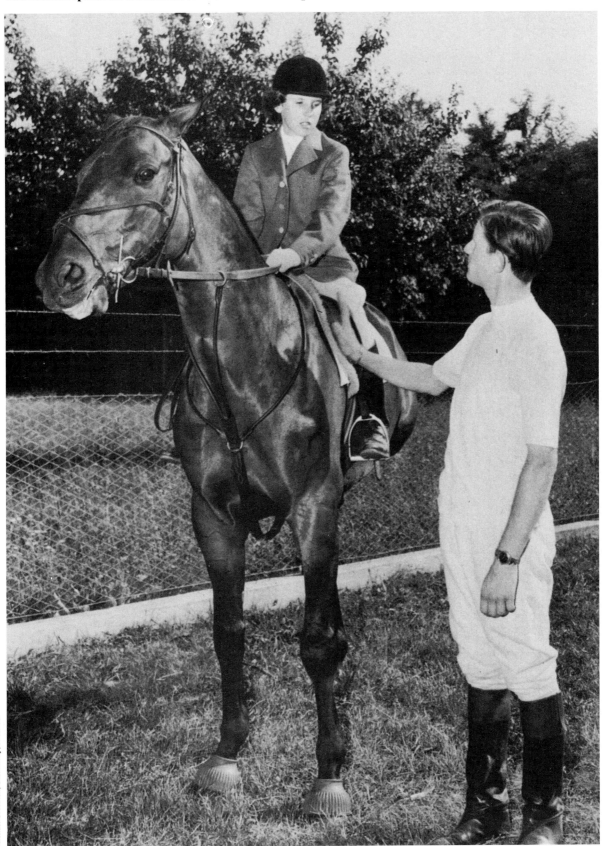

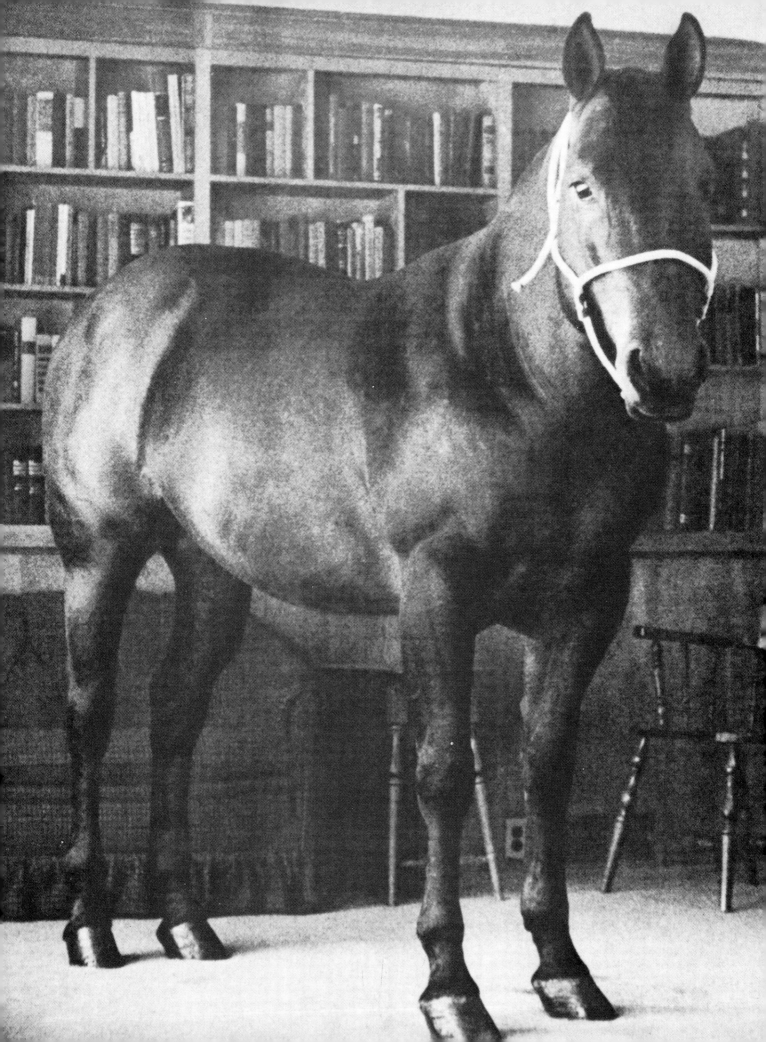

Just Browsing, Thanks

Inside the house to get duded up for a show, Josie's Twist wanders into the library to look for his fodder.

When Muzzle isn't pulling a bakery cart, he's scanning the sidewalks of New York from his high-rise stable.

Stretch in the Sun

Timber smiles over his pasturized life in Connecticut.

Michael J. Phillips,

Colt with a Hang-Up

In Sequim, Washington, Mischief decides to go AWOL but gets only halfway there.

Dagnie DeNoma, 3/22/68

Ponytails

**Paulette Tanulet feels somewhat upstaged
by a New York taxidermist's sample.**

Warren E. Siegmond. 9/29/58

This girl's palomino pal has a hair-raising similarity.

Nathan Jones, 8/1/69

The Horsey Set

Susan Molesworth is outmugged by her mount.

Shhh! It's the boss's son.

In Joplin, Missouri, a trusty steed helps pass the tools.

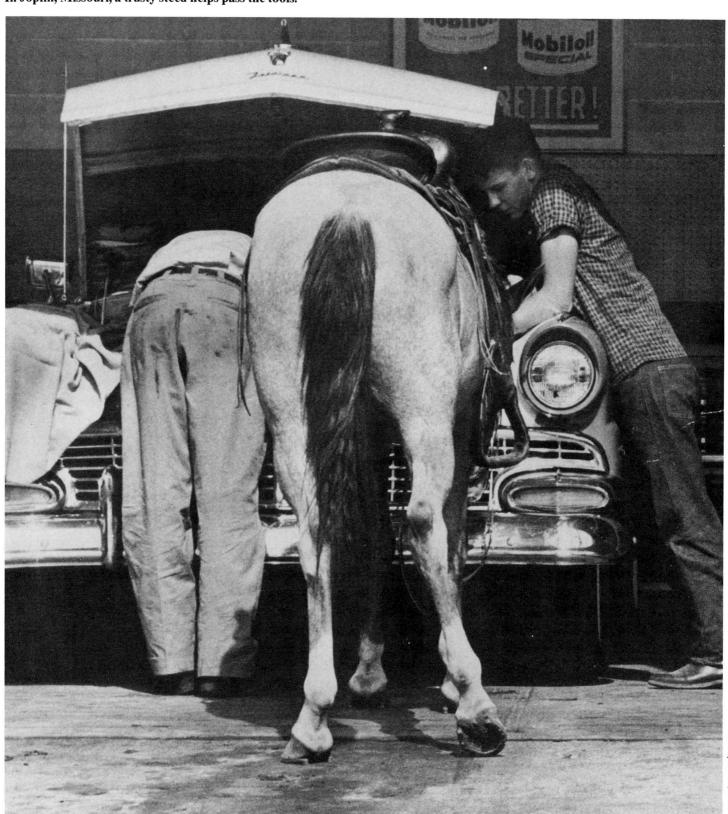

"Not That One— the Monkey Wrench!"

Outside Washington, D.C., assistance is proffered by a horse of a different color.

Chapter 12
Bids a Fond
Farewell
with This
MIXED BAG

Big Bender

In the Cheyenne Mountain zoo at Colorado
Springs, a contortionist named Pat limbers up.

About Town

This sharp operator is trying to make a deposit in Missoula's
First National. It turns out it's after hours and the prickly
customer has to wait till morning for his no-account bank to open.

John Wummer, 12/8/67

Stan Healy, Missoulian, 2/2/59

Gurgly Face-Off

**Nine-month-old Janet Stringer deals with some drifting
soap bubbles her father is blowing near by.**

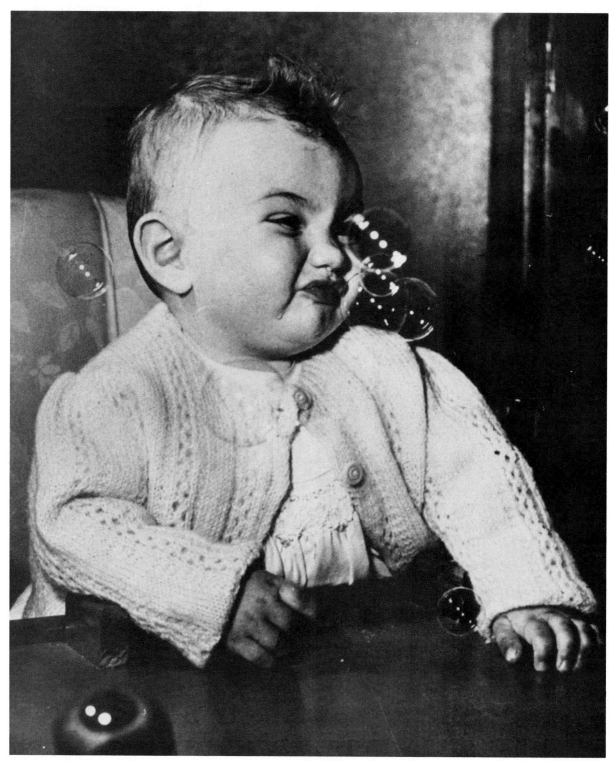

Tom Lyons, *London Daily Mirror*, 11/2/53

You can always lead a horse to water but here,
in California, water's being led to horse.

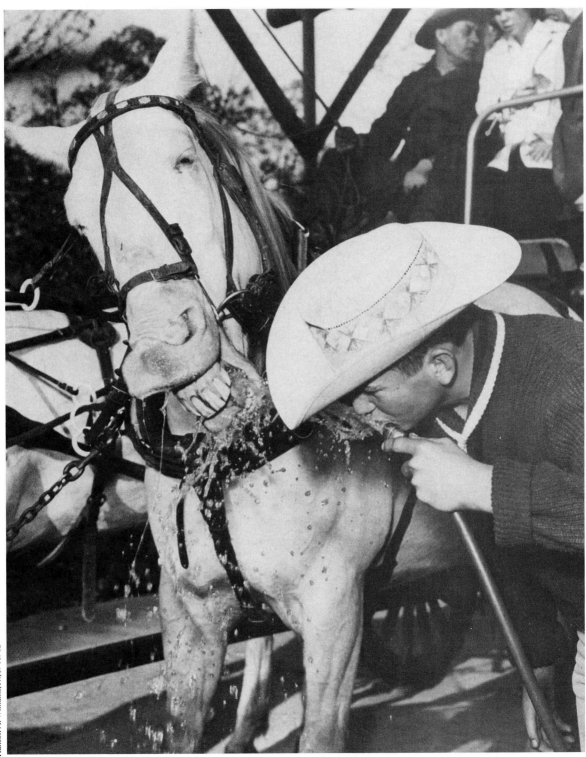

Hanson A. Williams, Jr., 5/18/62

Charming Pipers

On his new bamboo flute, twelve-year-old David Ranck of Strasburg, Pennsylvania, plays *Three Blind Mice* to three insightful heifers.

Harry M. Hess 6/21/63

**For this street piper in Lyons, France,
charming snakes or passersby is a lead-pipe cinch.**

Rene Mallete, Black Star, 7/5/63

Easy Pickings

A New York pigeon with his bill in the till.

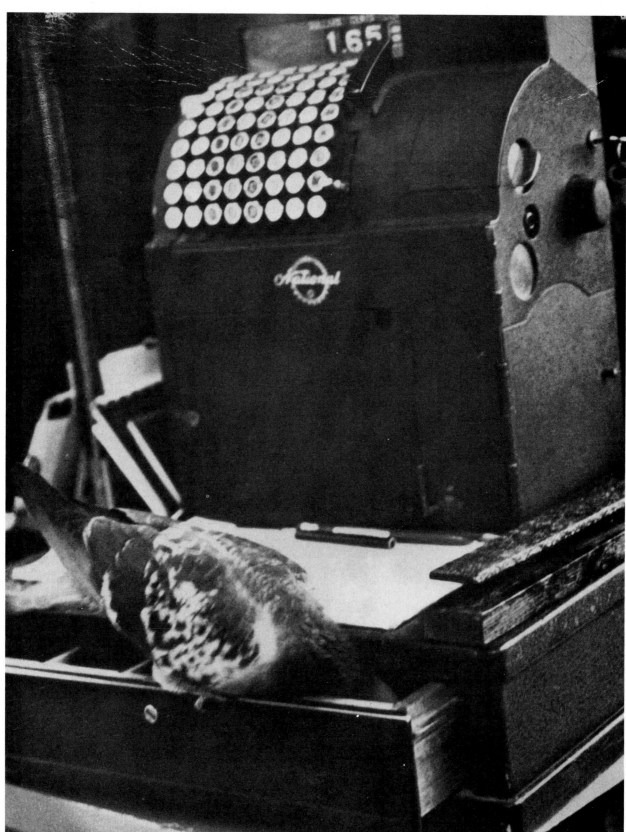

A New Jersey janitor's lazy Susan.

Bill Hirschmann, 12/1/67

Drivers' Ed

Washington, D.C.—where else?

Simon Goldsmith, 10/20/67

Switched to a siding.

Robert R. Taylor, 9/27/68

Motorists Who Care

Two-and-a-half-year-old Brian Noble strides away from his perfectly parked automobile.

Bob Noble, *New York Herald Tribune*, 5/24/63

Art Shay, 11/8/68

**No matter how hard
Steve Shay pulls
down, the garage door
wants to go up.**

Adoring Companions

In Chicago, the Ryan family is joined by friendship.

Bettmann/UPI, 8/31/62

This chimp only has eyes for his enraptured friend—and her cone.

John Drysdale, *Camera Press*, 8/18/67

That's All, Folks!

Dorothy Semorile, 12/15/6